Gainsboro[ugh]

on old picture po[stcards]

Eric Croft

1. The Old Hall. Any article or book on Gainsborough must feature this building, but it is impossible to describe in the few lines available here. It would need a book to itself, so why not pay it a visit? This postcard was published by the Friends of the Old Hall in the 1950's, and posted to Grimsby in April 1955.

*Designed and published by
Reflections of a Bygone Age,
Keyworth, Nottingham 2000*

*Printed by Adlard Print
& Reprographics Ltd*

INTRODUCTION

GAINSBOROUGH is a market town on the eastern bank of the River Trent, 18 miles north-west of Lincoln, with a long and fascinating history. Alfred The Great was married here in the year 868. It was invaded and devastated in 1013 under Sweyn, King of the Danes, and his son Canute. Sweyn is thought to be buried here, whilst Canute, later King Canute, supposedly bid the Aegir to leave the town!

It was probably a dangerous place to live during the Civil War. Being an important crossing point of the River Trent, it witnessed many battles and was held alternately by the Royalists and Parliamentarians on more than one occasion.

The most interesting and important building in the town is the Old Hall, rebuilt in 1470 and extended about 1600. Described as one of the most extensive and perfect examples of an ancient mansion, it is open to the public and must be visited.

The town was the home of Marshall, Sons & Co., manufacturers of traction engines, tractors and threshing machines. As you will see from the many postcards featuring the company, it was until recent years the major employer. It would perhaps be only a slight exaggeration to call it a 'company town'. The other major employer, Rose Brothers, is known throughout the country! They were makers of packaging machinery for the confectionery industry and particularly for Cadburys. So your "Roses" chocolates, though they may have a rose on the box, were in fact named after Rose Brothers to commemorate their association with Cadburys! Considering the vast number of "Marshall's" cards, it is strange that I have not yet found a postcard relating to Rose Bros.

In researching this book, when not pounding the streets I could be found in Jennifer Hall's antique shop, pestering her and her assistant Cuthbert Jackson for information. Mrs Argent-Cook from W.H. Smith was also most encouraging about my project. I thank them for their time, and also other local people, including the staff of Barnes the Jewellers.

The first picture postcard in Britain was published in 1894, but it was not until a decade later that they began to take off, when in 1902 the Post Office allowed a message to be written on the address side. This meant that the whole of one side was available for the picture, and this obviously gave more scope to the publishers. Photographic viewcards became very popular, and a national craze by 1905 saw the postcard become the most important way of communicating news or messages, in much the same way as the telephone is used today. The years up to 1914 were the "Golden Age" of picture postcards, when countless millions of imaginative designs, covering every subject under the sun, were published by a host of national and local firms. There's hardly a village or hamlet that wasn't documented at that time by a postcard publisher. Postcard collecting declined after World War I, but is once again a growing hobby, with increasing numbers of people taking up this absorbing interest.

Fortunately for us today, Gainsborough was well covered by postcard publishers, both local and national. Where known, these publishers are credited in the captions.

Eric Croft
March 2000

Front cover: River Trent. This postcard was published by Boots in their 'Real Photographic' series and whilst it is not a scarce card, it is one of my favourite Gainsborough cards and features one of the Trent ferry boats.

Back cover (top): Lord Street, Gainsborough, on Edwardian days.
    (bottom): The Great Central Railway Station (when it had a roof!) on a W.H. Smith card, posted to Lincoln in March 1910.

2. Lea Road. This card should really be captioned *'Gainsborough Road, Lea!'* The photographer was, however, stood on the boundary and looking towards Lea. The postcard was published by Lilywhite of Halifax.

3. Great Northern Railway Station, Lea Road, on a Doncaster Rotophoto Co. card posted in 1921. The station is still in use, and except for the loss of the iron railings it doesn't look any different today.

GREAT NORTHERN RAILWAY STATION, GAINSBOROUGH.

4. Another view of the station, but this postcard was published by W.H. Smith about 1908. The road is a little wider and a great deal busier, and the card features a time when driving down the middle of the road was not a problem.

LEA ROAD, GAINSBOROUGH.

5. Lea Road. Another view of the road that has hardly changed. The large tree has gone, together with the telephone poles. The card, another Lilywhite production, was posted in 1927.

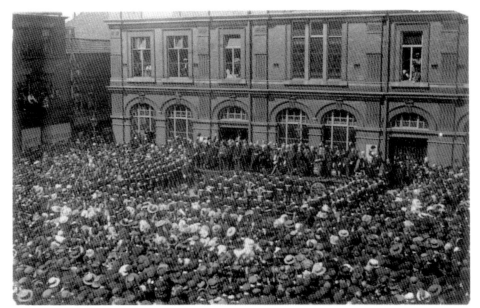

6. The Market Place. This card was posted in Gainsborough on 15th May 1910 and the message tells us it is the proclamation of the new king, George V. It goes on to read "... *the weather is grand and very hot. Wonder if it's on account of the comet?*"

7. The Market Place, but this time the crowd was gathered for Peace Day celebrations on 19th July 1919. I can't see a single person who is not wearing a hat of some sort! The card was produced by local photographer Mr D. Harris.

8. Pillared House, situated on Bridge Street, was built in 1670. Regrettably, it was demolished in 1936 and the only reminder of it is the modern group dwelling building nearby called Pillard House. Postcard publishers must have looked on it as an important building or a curiosity, because cards of the building are quite common. This card was published by the Doncaster Rotophoto Co.

9. Northolme on a card published by W.F. Belton, posted to Kings Lynn in September 1906. The ivy has gone but little else has changed. The houses face Gainsborough Trinity football ground.

10. Holy Trinity Church Institute on a card posted in July 1908. The building, minus the roof lantern, and the adjoining houses have survived. Holy Trinity Church in the background is now an Arts Centre.

11. King's Theatre, a wonderful building dating from 1885 and originally called the Albert Hall. It is remarkably intact, and even the lion retains its tail! The building is now daubed in brick-red and white paint and has a distinctly derelict look. Surely a building worth preserving and eligible for some Lottery funds?

THE RADICAL CURE FOR UNEMPLOYMENT

    DOWN WITH THE LORDS.
    DOWN WITH THE CONSTITUTION.
    DOWN WITH THE CHURCH.
    DOWN WITH THE CATHOLICS.
    DOWN WITH THE PUBLICANS.
    DOWN WITH THE ENGLISH LANDOWNER.
    DOWN WITH THE ENGLISH CAPITALIST.
    and
    UP WITH THE FOREIGNER.

Vote for Henderson

 AND BRITISH WORK
FOR BRITISH HANDS

Printed by C. Caldicott, Market Place, Gainsborough, and published by R. F. Neave, 37, Market Street, Gainsborough.

12. This is an electioneering card from the early years of the century, with the Conservative candidate scaremongering over alleged Liberal Party policies.

13. Mr Wright, the rag and bone man, in Etherington Street on a card posted in 1906. At least one of his cart wheels was once part of a mangle, but neither the cart or donkey, nor even Mr Wright, look to be in the best of health! There is at least one similar card of Mr Wright with his donkey.

14. Men leaving Marshall's works. I don't know why the photographers of the period were so interested in these shots, but there are several, including some by the large postcard publishers. This one was published by Soloman Bros. and posted in August 1917 to Larbert in Stirlingshire.

15. Same theme, but this picture was taken at the junction of Southolme, Trinity Street and Beaumont Street. The houses have survived, but everything to the right hand side has gone and a supermarket is being built on the site. Card published by Valentine of Dundee, and posted to Lincoln in May 1910.

16. Marshall's Britannia works c. 1905. This shows part of the new boiler shop, and is one of a series of interior views of the factory.

17. A view of Marshall's offices on a card posted to Fulstow in September 1904. The title includes the information that the works employed 3,600 men and covered 28 acres. This building is now the home of the town's Heritage Centre. The statue of Britannia is still in place, but the Royal coat of arms has gone.

18. A Marshall boiler being hauled by elephants in Ceylon, again one of a series of similar cards depicting Ceylon scenes. I assume Marshalls imported them for advertising purposes.

19. The funeral procession of Mr H.D. Marshall on 15th March 1906 was featured on many cards by several publishers. This photograph shows the procession on Lea Road about to pass under the railway bridge.

20. The fire at Marshalls on 6th May 1914. Judging by the crowds, this photograph must have been taken soon after the event. There are at least five men with wheelbarrows full of bricks. I wonder what they were doing?

21. The final resting place of Mr H.D.Marshall. His lifelong engineering background followed him to his grave, as one of the wreaths is in the shape of a spoked wheel. The card was posted from Sturton by Stow to Gonalston in July 1907.

22. Lea Road School on a card posted at Broughton in December 1906. The building looks exactly the same today, but is no longer a school. It closed a few years ago and is now used as office accommodation by several companies.

23. Queen Elizabeth Grammar School on a 1960's postcard. This view is also unchanged, but this school is very much in use!

24. The "Mill on the floss" takes its name from George Elliot's novel of that title, and postcards of it are quite common, and invariably include Gainsborough in the title. The mill was, however, in the neighbouring parish of Morton and the book is, in any case, a work of fiction. I believe other mills in neighbouring counties also claim to be the "Mill on the floss".

25. A decorated float on a card published by local photographer C.W. Stephenson. It is not dated or used and is therefore a bit of a mystery! The men's sashes carry the letters NUFO/C with varying other letters but the children's sashes are of a different design. The uniform of the sergeant (2nd from left) looks like a police uniform but with a railway company cap!

26. The coronation of George VI in 1937. As the card is just over 60 years old, perhaps a lot of the children on the front rows are still with us! The card was published by local photographer Frank S. Wilson.

27. Yet another street procession! This is the Nurse's Carnival on a card by Gainsborough photographer D. Girdlestone and posted in July 1911. The message begins *"Hope the heat has not quite killed you - it really is very upsetting!"*

28. Another procession, another photographer! This is the British Legion Carnival in 1923, and the photographer this time was a Mr. J. Glover of Gainsborough.

29. Gainsborough Show on a card posted in the town on 1st August 1906 to Banbury. Quite an impressive event, by the look of the trade park and band stand.

30. Lord Street on a Jackson's of Grimsby postcard c. 191
picture, and, judging by the number of people, it was on m
corn binder for sale. I wonder if they sold it!

photographer was standing in Market Street to take this
...y. Note the mobile office of Edlingtons on the left and a

31. Gainsborough railway disaster c.1912. There are at least six views of this disaster, but all seem to be quite scarce. It would appear that only one train was involved, but it damaged the signal box and a signal gantry. The tarpaulin covering the threshing machine is lettered in Russian. Was this a Marshall export that didn't get very far?

32. This view of the accident shows teddy bears scattered about. I wonder if they were exports or imports, and what would a truck load of them be worth today?

33. This postcard shows the opening of the John Coupland Hospital in 1913. The townspeople certainly liked their processions and similar events. I wonder how big the crowd would be these days!

34. Howard Welchman published both these cards and he got the name right on this one - it *is* Coupland! *(note the spelling on illus. 33).*

35. The Constitutional Club Committee in 1911 photographed by Welchman. What a humourless looking bunch - even the dog looks bored stiff!

36. I am not sure of the location, but the card was posted in Gainsborough in December 1904 and was addressed to Mr M. Robinson, no.2 steamroller driver, East Ferry. The roadroller was, of course, made by Marshalls.

37. The Parish Church of All Saints on an undated postcard, but from a time when it had iron railings! The trees have also gone, but I think the open aspect is more attractive. Why were churches so keen on keeping people out? The churchyard residents certainly didn't need fencing in!

JOHN ROBINSON MEMORIAL CHURCH, GAINSBOROUGH

38. The John Robinson Memorial Church next door to the parish church (John Robinson was the pastor to the Pilgrim Fathers). The building is largely unchanged, except that it has also lost its railings and the decorative emblem from the gable. It is now the United Reformed Church. This card was published by Beckett of Gainsborough, and posted to Thetford in July 1912.

39. Trinity Street. This is another card published by Belton and it was posted in 1908. Mr Atkinson's grocery shop continued in business for many years and it was noted for the smell of roasting coffee beans. Whilst it is no longer a grocers, the building is unchanged.

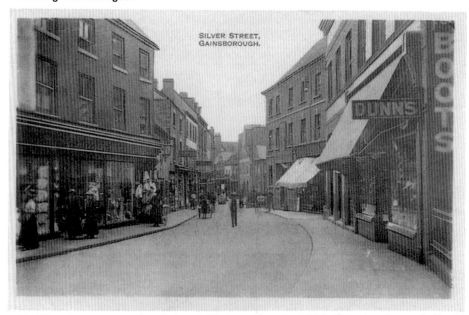

40. Silver Street on another Solomon Bros. postcard c.1910. This view looks similar today, although many of the shops have been rebuilt over the years. The buildings in the distance are actually in Bridge Street.

41. Market Street. During the Second World War, a bombing raid on the town destroyed most of the buildings on the right, and the remainder were later demolished and the site redeveloped. A local character expressed the opinion that the developers did more damage than the bombs! Card published by Valentine of Dundee, and posted from Spalding to Saxilby in March 1910.

42. Highfield. The mill tower has survived - just. Without windows or even a roof, it looks a very sorry sight. A 'Kingsway' series postcard published by W.H. Smith.

43. Church Street. This postcard is not dated or postally used, but was probably published by Jackson of Grimsby c.1910. The scene has changed dramatically, as all or most of the buildings have been replaced! The photographer was standing near the junction of Gladstone Street, facing the market area.

44. Hawthorne Avenue on a Lilywhite postcard. At first glance these houses give the impression of a 1950's design, but here they are on a card posted in 1927!

45. Morton Terrace on a Lilywhite's postcard posted in 1942, but probably dating from the 1920's. This view is pretty much the same today, apart from the traffic, as it is one of the main thoroughfares.

46. The Aegir (or Eagre). There are perhaps hundreds of similar views of the Aegir, but this one with the barges ploughing through it is more interesting than most. The photographer was Brocklehurst of Gainsborough, and it was posted in 1911. For the benefit of 'foreigners', the Aegir is a tidal wave or bore, and it can be quite dramatic, rising to a height of several feet on the Spring tides.

47. I know very little about this postcard. It shows the Salvation Army band playing on board a Trent ferry boat, and was published by yet another local photographer, C.E. Seneschal.

48. Market Hall. This would be better titled Lord Street, as the only connection with the market is the arched doorway on the right, and it opened onto a staircase leading up to the first floor of the Town Hall. The gas light on the right is at the entrance to the pathway leading to the Market Square and quaintly named Flag Alley. Postcard published by Valentine about 1912.

49. Tower Street on a card posted in 1905. The shop is now a house, the children must now be very old and the horse manure has been swept up, otherwise it is much the same! If the photographer had faced the opposite way, the name would have been obvious, as the church tower is in line with the street.

50. Spital Terrace featured on a card posted to Miss Parker of Morton Terrace in 1906. The message is *"Do you recognise your former abode?"* I would think she did, as the two streets are within five minutes walking distance! The street looks the same today, except for the hideous modern lamp columns!

51. The Post Office on a W.H. Smith card c.1910. They liked building post offices in Gainsborough! This one lasted only a few years before another one was built next door, but that has now closed and the latest one is "buried" in the new Co-op shop!

52. The "White Horse Inn" on Silver Street on a postcard sent by Mr. Wilson, the landlord, in 1906. In his message he claims the inn is 500 years old. I think he has added a century or two! It has now been 'Tudorised,' complete with timbers and bow windows.

SEVEN STARS WHARF, GAINSBOROUGH.

53. Part of the town's river frontage on a card posted in 1913 and includes the message *"...and have been passed again on the river; could not land us again while the tide came!"* ?? Most, if not all, of these warehouses have been rebuilt over the years, but the whole area is now to be redeveloped. Card published by Solomon Brothers of London.

54. Town Hall and Market Place. The former was built in 1892 and was rather grand for the size of the town. Unfortunately, it suffered some bomb damage during the war, and the front facade was rebuilt. It is in plain red brick and of austere design. The ground floor (now shops) has an even more modern frontage, but this is partly hidden by a 1980's canopy. To complete the modernisation, the new Town Hall clock is hung on the side of the building! Ugh!

BRIDGE ROAD WESLEYAN CHURCH, GAINSBOROUGH.

55. Bridge Road Methodist Church on yet another of Belton's postcards. The church was demolished about thirty years ago.

56. One of the famous Belton's shops. This one was situated in Market Street, on the corner opposite the entrance to the Market Place. The shop advertised pens, and the area became known as 'pen corner.' This postcard is not dated, but whatever the year, they were stocked up for Christmas. The window includes diaries, childrens' annuals and *'post early for Christmas'* notices.